MW01232859

GAYLORD R

Animals in Their Habitats

Wetland Animals

Francine Galko

Heinemann Library
Chicago, Illinois

Designed by Ginkgo Creative
Printed and bound in the United States by Lake Book Manufacturing, Inc.

07 06 05 04 03
10 9 8 7 6 5 4 3 2 1

Library of Congress Cataloging-in-Publication Data

Galko, Francine.
     Wetland animals / Francine Galko.
          p. cm. — (Animals in their habitats)
Includes bibliographical references (p.   ).
Summary: Describes wetlands, the different kinds of animals that can be
found in them, and their ecological importance.
     ISBN 1-40340-186-1 (HC), 1-4034-0443-7 (Pbk.)
     1. Wetland animals—Juvenile literature. [1. Wetlands. 2. Wetland animals. 3. Wetland ecology. 4. Ecology.]
     QL113.8 .G25 2002
     591.768—dc21
                              2001007650

Acknowledgments
The author and publishers are grateful to the following for permission to reproduce copyright material:
Cover photograph by Willard Luce/Animals Animals
p. 4 Eastcott/Momatiuk/Animals Animals; p. 5 C. C. Lockwood/Animals Animals; p. 6 Tui de Roy/Bruce Coleman Inc.; p. 7
Erwin and Peggy Bauer; p. 8 Rick Poley; p. 9 Jack Dermid/Visuals Unlimited; p. 10 Phil Dotson/Photo Researchers, Inc.; p. 11
C. C. Lockwood/Bruce Coleman Inc.; p. 12 Lynn M. Stone/Bruce Coleman Inc.; p. 13 Willard Luce/Animals Animals; p. 14 Zig
Leszczynski/Animals Animals; p. 15 Bruce Coleman Inc.; p. 16 Eleanor Osborn; p. 17 S. Nielsen/Bruce Coleman Inc.; p. 18
Harry Engels/Animals Animals; p. 19 Hans Reinhard/Bruce Coleman Inc.; p. 20 Ken Cole/Animals Animals; p. 21 Robert
Maier/Animals Animals; p. 22 Roger Rageot/David Liebman; p. 23 Nada Pecnik/Visuals Unlimited; p. 24 Bill Beatty/Animals
Animals; p. 25 Joe McDonald/Bruce Coleman Inc.; p. 26 Marie Read/Animals Animals; p. 27 E. R. Degginger/Animals Animals;
p. 28 Dell Metzen/Bruce Coleman Inc.; p. 29 Steve Oulett/Bruce Coleman Inc.
Every effort has been made to contact copyright holders of any material reproduced in this book. Any omissions will be
rectified in subsequent printings if notice is given to the publisher.

Some words are shown in bold, **like this.** You can find out what they mean by looking in the glossary.

To learn more about the avocet on the cover, turn to page 13.

Contents

What is a Wetland?

A wetland is a kind of **habitat**. It is wet, soft land. Like a soggy sponge, the land is usually full of water. **Swamps** and **marshes** are wetlands.

Some wetlands hold **fresh water**. Often trees grow in these wetlands. Other wetlands hold salt water from the oceans or seas. Usually grasses grow in these wetlands.

Where are Wetlands?

Wetlands are all over the world. They are near oceans, rivers, lakes, and forests. Some wetlands dry up part of the year. Other wetlands freeze in winter.

Wetlands are anywhere water stays in or on top of the land. The water is not very deep. An adult can touch the bottom when standing up tall in the water.

Wetland Homes

Wetlands have many homes for animals. The apple snail, **insects,** and other animals live in the water. Some animals live along the edge of the water.

Lugworms live in the mud. When a lugworm moves through the mud, it sometimes leaves a long tube of mud behind. These mud tubes are called **wormcasts**.

Living in the Water

A congo eel **protects** her eggs from danger at the bottom of a **swamp.** The young eels will live in the same swamp. Congo eels are really salamanders with very tiny legs.

During the day, crayfish hide in the mud at the bottom of a swamp. At night, they come out of the mud. Sometimes they even leave the water.

Living on the Edge of the Water

Many animals live near the water. The Florida panther climbs in trees and hunts beside the water. It eats deer, raccoons, and even small alligators.

Wetlands have many different kinds of birds. Avocets make their nests near the water. They find food in the mud and water of the wetland.

Living in the Mud

Some animals live in the mud. The spadefoot toad digs backwards into the mud. Each of its back feet is shaped like a special shovel. It usually hides in its mud hole most of the day.

Star-nosed moles dig long tunnels in the mud. They spend most of their time under the ground. The mole's nose helps it find food in the mud.

Wetland Territories

Animals find food and **mates** near their homes. The place around an animal's home is its **territory.** These two wood ducks are deciding who will win this territory.

Animals often fight with each other over a territory. Muskrats will fight hard to **protect** their territory. As many as ten muskrats might live in one **den**.

Finding Food in a Wetland

Wetlands have many plants and animals to eat. Some animals find food in the water. In summer, moose wade into the water and eat wetland plants.

Some wetland animals eat other wetland animals. Raccoons catch fishes, frogs, crabs, and **insects** near the edge of the water. They wash their food before eating it.

Wetland Predators

Many wetland animals are **predators**. They hunt other animals in the wetland. Anhingas are great hunters. They dive into the water and catch fish.

Minks are also wetland predators. They use their sharp teeth to catch **prey**. Minks eat mice, birds, and fishes.

When a Wetland is Dry

Sometimes a wetland dries up. During a **drought,** some salamanders move into the mud. This salamander can live in the mud for two months without drying out.

Alligators dig holes with their tail. The holes hold water during a drought. Alligators eat the other animals that come to drink from the water hole.

Hiding in a Wetland

Camouflage is one way to hide from **predators.** The spots on this newt look like small rocks. The newt blends into the wetland rocks and land.

This water moccasin snake is almost the same color as the water. It's easy for this snake to hide from the birds and other **reptiles** that like to eat it.

Wetland Babies

Wetlands have many places for animals to have babies. Marsh wrens build nests in the **reeds**.

Baby snapping turtles hatch from eggs on land. When they grow up, snapping turtles live in the water.

Protecting Wetland Animals

People did not always like wetlands.
Wetlands have a lot of mosquitoes. It's hard
to build on the wet ground. Sometimes
people **drain** wetlands, so they can build
houses and parking lots.

Today, people work to keep wetlands safe and clean for the animals and plants that live there. Sometimes people put water back into wetlands that were drained. Then the wetland animals come back.

Glossary

camouflage way an animal hides itself

drain take the water out

drought when no rain falls for a long time

fresh water water from lakes, streams, ponds; water that is not salty

habitat place where an animal lives

insect small animal with six legs

larva (more than one are called larvae) very young insect

mate animal that an animal will make babies with

marsh kind of wetland with grasses and no trees

predator animal that hunts and eats other animals

prey animal that is hunted and eaten by another animal

protects keeps safe

reeds wetland plants that look like very tall grasses

reptile member of a group of animals that includes snakes, lizards, and turtles

swamp kind of wetland usually covered with water and trees

territory place around an animal's home

wormcast long tube of mud left behind when a lugworm moves through the mud

More Books to Read

Arnosky, Jim. *Crinkleroot's Guide to Knowing Animal Habitats.* New York: Aladdin Picture Books, 1998.

Fowler, Allan. *Life in a Wetland.* Danbury, Conn.: Children's Press, 1999.

Gibbons, Gail. *Marshes & Swamps.* New York: Holiday House, 1999.

Index